Egermeier's
Bible Storybook
for Beginners

®

Belongs to

_____

Egermeier's Bible Storybook for Beginners

Stories by Elsie Egermeier
Story Revisions by Robin Fogle
Illustrations by Pat Paris

82997018253

Text ©2012 Warner Press Inc.

Illustrations ©2012 by Pat Paris

ISBN: 978-1-59317-426-2

Published by Warner Press, Inc, 1201 E. 5th Street, Anderson, IN 46012

Author: Elsie Egermeier
Story Revisions: Robin Fogle
Illustrations: Pat Paris
Design Layout: Kevin Spear
Editors: Robin Fogle, Karen Rhodes

Printed in China

Contents

Old Testament

Contents

New Testament

How the World Was Made

Genesis 1:1—2:24

Long, long ago there was no world at all. There was no sun to shine, no stars to twinkle, no moonbeams to play through the night shadows. But even then there was God, for He has always been the same unchanging God.

Then, at the beginning of time, God made the world. At first water covered everything, and darkness was everywhere. But God planned to make it beautiful, so He said, "Let there be light." He called the light Day and the darkness Night. This was the first day.

On the second day God made the beautiful blue sky and clouds. He called the sky Heaven.

The third day God said, "Let the waters gather together in one place, and let the dry land appear." He called the waters Seas and the dry land Earth. The whole earth was bare—no grasses, flowers or trees. So God caused a carpet of grass to grow and colorful flowers to spring up from the ground. He made the trees and plants. God knew His work was good.

But God had more plans for His world. On the fourth day He made the sun, moon and stars. The sun was to rule the day and the moon, the night.

Next God created all kinds of fish to swim in the seas and birds to fly in the sky. The fifth day passed, and the world had become a better place.

On the sixth day God said, "Let the earth produce living creatures." Every kind of animal and living thing appeared in the woods and fields, in the deserts and on the mountains.

Still the world seemed strange. There were no homes anywhere—not a man, woman or little child. But God had not finished creating His wonderful world yet. He planned to make people to live on the earth, to enjoy it and take care of it. They would know who had made all these things, and they would be able to love and worship Him.

So God decided to make the first man. Out of the dust of the earth, He made the body. Then He breathed into that body the breath of life. Man became a living soul.

God called the first man Adam. Adam got to name the birds and animals. His job was to rule over all other living creatures.

Now Adam needed a helper. God said, "It is not good for man to be alone." So God made Adam a wife, and Adam loved her very much. He called his wife Eve.

When the sixth day ended God had made the world and everything in it, just as He had planned. On the seventh day God rested.

Adam and Eve
Genesis 2:8—3:24

Adam and Eve were very happy in their garden home. God had given them good things to enjoy, and they knew nothing about evil and wrongdoing. God walked with them in the cool evenings.

In this garden God planted a wonderful tree called the tree of life. Whoever ate the fruit of this tree would live forever. Another tree was called the tree of knowledge of good and evil. God said, "You may eat the fruit of every tree in the garden except from the tree of the knowledge of good and evil. If you eat of this tree, you will surely die."

One day the serpent asked Eve, "Will God let you eat the fruit of every tree in this garden?"

"We may eat of every tree except one," Eve answered. "God told us not to eat of the tree of knowledge of good and evil, or we will die."

"You will not die," the serpent replied. "God knows that if you eat fruit from this tree you will become as wise as He is. That is why He told you not to eat it."

Eve looked at the fruit. If it would really make her wise like God, she wanted to taste it. Reaching out her hand, she picked the fruit, ate it, and gave some to Adam. He ate the fruit too.

At once Adam and Eve knew they had disobeyed God. Fear filled their hearts. They had never been afraid before, but now they tried to find a hiding place among the beautiful trees in the garden. Their hearts had become wicked.

Soon a voice called, "Adam, where are you?"

Adam answered, "Lord, I heard Your voice and I was afraid, so I hid."

"Why should you be afraid of Me?" God asked. "Have you eaten the forbidden fruit?"

Adam said, "Eve gave me some of the fruit, and I ate it."

"What have you done?" God asked Eve.

She answered, "The serpent tempted me and I ate."

God's heart was very sad because Adam and Eve had disobeyed Him. Now they could no longer be with Him because sin had spoiled their lives. They could not live in the beautiful garden God had made for them anymore.

God sent them out into the world to make their own home. He placed an angel at the garden gate so Adam and Eve could never come back to eat of the tree of life.

God said to Eve, "Because you have disobeyed Me, you will have pain and trouble."

God punished Adam too. No longer would it be easy to grow fruits and vegetables. Weeds, thorns and thistles would grow in his fields.

When Adam and Eve died, their bodies would become dust again. All this came because of sin.

Noah's Ark
Genesis 5:1—9:17

As the years passed there were more and more people in the world. Most of them were very wicked. How sorry God was that He had made people! Finally God decided the only way to get rid of sin and wickedness in the world was to cover the earth with a huge flood.

Then God remembered Noah. Noah tried to do right, and he taught his sons to do right too. This made God happy.

Sometimes God talked to Noah. Now He told Noah about His plan to destroy the world. He promised Noah and his family that they would not be destroyed with the wicked people.

"Build an ark," God told Noah. "When it is finished you and your wife and your sons and their wives will go into the ark. You will live there until the flood is over."

God decided to save two of each kind of living thing. These would also stay in the ark during the flood.

Because Noah believed God, he began building the ark. God told him how to build it. The ark looked like a three-story houseboat perched up on dry land.

How the people must have laughed at Noah and his three sons! Where was the water for their boat? Again and

again Noah warned the people they would be destroyed in the flood if they were not sorry for their sins. None of them believed him.

When everything was ready, God told Noah to take his wife, his three sons and their wives into the ark. Then God caused two of every kind of animal, bird and creeping thing to go into the ark. Seven pairs of each kind of useful birds and animals came. When all were inside, God shut the door.

After a few days the rain began to fall. And such a rain! Water poured down from the clouds. Soon the rivers were overflowing. People left their homes and rushed to the hills for safety. Animals ran pell-mell, trying to find shelter. Still it rained. Higher and higher the waters rose. Now the people knew Noah had told the truth.

For forty days and nights it rained. Only Noah and his family were safe. The waters lifted the ark off the ground. For more than six months it floated. Then one day it stood still on top of a mountain.

After a while, Noah opened a window and let out a raven. This bird had strong wings and could fly around until the waters had gone down. Several days later Noah sent out a dove. The dove returned because she could not find a place to build her nest. A week later Noah sent the dove out again. She stayed longer this time. When evening came, she flew back, bringing a green olive leaf in her mouth. Now Noah and his family knew the land was becoming green and beautiful. The next week when Noah sent out the dove, she flew away and never came back.

Finally God said to Noah, "Come out of the ark with your family and every living thing that is in the ark."

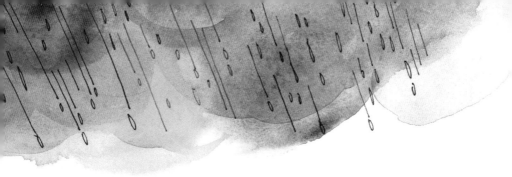

Noah opened the large door. He and his family stepped out on dry ground. All the animals, the birds and the creeping things came out too.

Noah was thankful to be alive. As soon as he came out of the ark, he built an altar and made his offering to God. God was pleased with Noah and his family.

God promised that He would never again send another flood to destroy every living creature. God said, "As long as the earth remains there will be summer and winter, springtime and autumn, and day and night." To remind people of His promise, God made the rainbow in the sky.

Joseph and His Colorful Coat

Genesis 37

Jacob had twelve sons, but he loved his son Joseph the most. When Jacob made a wonderful coat of many colors for Joseph, the older sons were jealous. They hated their brother.

One day Joseph saw four of his brothers do wrong. As soon as he could he told his father. They hated Joseph even more for telling on them.

One night Joseph had a strange dream. He told his brothers about it. "We were together in the field, tying up bundles of grain. My bundle stood up tall, and yours bowed down around it."

How angry the brothers were! "Do you think you will rule over us someday?" they asked.

Soon Joseph dreamed again. He told his father and brothers, "In my dream I saw the sun, the moon and eleven stars bowing down before me."

Jacob said, "Do you think your mother, your brothers and I will bow down to you?" That dream seemed to make Joseph better than his whole family. Jacob wondered what such a dream could mean.

Jacob's flocks of cattle and sheep were very large. Sometimes the brothers had to take them far from home to find grass and water. This time Jacob sent them to Shechem. After they had been away for several weeks, Jacob sent Joseph to find out how they were.

When Joseph got to Shechem, he could not find his brothers and their flocks. A man from a nearby town told Joseph, "Your brothers have gone to Dothan to find better pasture."

Joseph journeyed on, over the hills and across the valleys. When the brothers saw a young man in a beautiful coat coming across the fields, they said, "Here comes the dreamer. Let's kill him and see what will become of his dreams."

Reuben, the oldest, did not want to hurt Joseph. He said, "Let's just throw him down into this pit and leave him alone to die." Reuben planned to rescue Joseph as soon as the others went away.

The brothers grabbed Joseph, tore off his beautiful coat and threw him into the pit. Paying no attention to Joseph's shouts, they sat down on the ground and ate lunch.

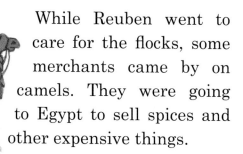

While Reuben went to care for the flocks, some merchants came by on camels. They were going to Egypt to sell spices and other expensive things.

"Now," thought Judah, "we can get rid of our brother and make some money!" He said, "It would be better to sell Joseph to these merchants than to let him die in the pit. Even though we hate him, he is our brother."

The others were happy to sell Joseph. They pulled him out of the pit and sold him to the merchants for twenty pieces of silver.

Poor Joseph! He was going to be taken far away by strangers. All his tears did not make any difference to his brothers. They divided the money and thought they were rid of Joseph forever.

When the merchants left, the brothers returned to their work, and Reuben hurried back to the pit. Stooping down, he called to Joseph. There was no answer. Again and again he called, but Joseph did not reply. He ran to his brothers. "The boy is gone! What am I going to do?" As the oldest Reuben felt responsible for his brother.

The brothers told Reuben what they had done. "But what will we tell our father about Joseph?" they wondered. Finally they decided to dip Joseph's coat in the blood of an animal, take the bloodstained coat to their father and tell him that they had found it.

When Jacob saw the blood-covered coat, he knew it was Joseph's. He believed wild animals had killed his son. Jacob was so sad that no one could comfort him.

A Baby and a Basket

Exodus 1:1—2:10

God's people were called Israelites. They lived in the land of Goshen, and their numbers grew until they became a strong nation.

Pharaoh, the king, was afraid of the Israelites. Pharaoh called his people together and said, "We must do something to stop the Israelites from becoming stronger and more powerful than we are."

He and his officers decided to make the Israelites their slaves. Pharaoh wanted new cities, and he made the Israelites build them. But the harder they worked, the stronger the Israelites became.

Pharaoh was even more afraid. "This will never do," he said. "I must make life even worse for them." And he did.

One morning Pharaoh sent the Israelites this message: "Every baby boy that is born to your people must be thrown into the Nile River."

Into such a world Moses was born. How much his mother loved him! For three months she hid him from the soldiers. Then the baby was too old to hide. So she gathered bulrushes that grew along the river and wove them into a basket. To keep the water out, she plastered the basket with pitch. Then she made a soft bed in the bottom.

Next came the very hardest part. She put the baby in the basket and carried the basket to the river. There among the tall reeds at the water's edge, she placed her precious basket and went home. Sister Miriam played along the riverbank and watched the basket.

Soon a group of richly dressed women came. One of them was the Egyptian princess, Pharaoh's daughter. They had come to bathe in the river. When the princess saw the strange-looking basket floating among the reeds, she sent her maid to get it.

"What can be inside this basket?" the women wondered as they gathered round to see it opened. How surprised they were to see a little baby! The baby was crying, and the princess lifted him lovingly.

"This is one of the Israelite's children," the princess said. She knew about her father's command, but how could she let this sweet little baby be killed? "I'll take him for my own," she decided.

When Miriam heard this, she ran to the princess and asked, "Would you like an Israelite woman to nurse this baby for you?" The princess was glad to hire an Israelite woman.

Miriam ran home and quickly brought her mother. How happy and thankful they were to carry the baby back home!

When the baby grew old enough to leave his mother, he was taken to live with the princess at Pharaoh's palace. The princess named him Moses, which means "drawn out," because she had drawn him out of the water.

God Speaks to Samuel

1 Samuel 1:1—3:18

Hannah was unhappy because she did not have any children. More than anything else, she wanted a baby.

When Hannah went with her husband to the tabernacle, she prayed, "Lord, if You will give me a baby boy, I will give him back to You to serve You the rest of his life."

Eli, the priest, saw Hannah. He noticed that her lips moved, but he did not hear a sound. He wondered what was wrong. Hannah explained, "I am very sad, and I have told the Lord the trouble."

"Go in peace," Eli told her, "and may the Lord give you what you have asked."

Hannah was not sad anymore. She knew the Lord had answered her prayer. Her heart was happy as she and her husband returned home.

Before another year passed, God gave Hannah a baby boy. Hannah named him Samuel, which means, "asked of God."

When Samuel was old enough, Hannah took him to Eli, the high priest. Hannah said, "I prayed for this child. Because the Lord answered my prayer, I have brought Samuel to help in the tabernacle. As long as he lives he will belong to the Lord."

Eli knew God was pleased with Hannah. He promised to take care of Samuel and teach him to serve God. Then Hannah and her husband went home.

Every year when Hannah and her husband came to the tabernacle, Hannah brought a new coat for Samuel. Each year she was glad to see how much taller he had grown, and she was thankful when Eli told her how Samuel helped in the tabernacle.

Eli had two sons who were priests. Even though Eli knew his sons did wrong, he still allowed them to serve at the tabernacle. He tried to get them to change their ways, but they would not listen.

Then God sent a prophet to warn Eli that his sons would be punished. Because Eli let them serve as priests, he would be punished too.

After the prophet went away, God spoke to Samuel one night. Samuel did not know it was God speaking. When he

heard a voice calling him, he thought it was Eli. Quickly
Samuel got out of bed and ran to Eli. "Here I am," he said,
and he waited for Eli to say what he wanted.

But Eli had not called Samuel. He said, "I did not call
you, my boy. Go back and lie down again." And Samuel
obeyed.

Soon the voice spoke again, "Samuel!" The boy rubbed his sleepy eyes and hurried to Eli's bedside.

"Here I am," he said. "I heard you call."

Again Eli told him, "I did not call. You may go back to bed."

The voice called Samuel a third time. When Samuel ran to Eli, the old man knew God wanted to speak to the boy. Eli said, "Go and lie down. If the voice calls you again, say, 'Speak, Lord, for Your servant listens.'"

Samuel went back and lay down again. Soon he heard the voice of God calling, "Samuel! Samuel!"

And the boy answered, "Speak, Lord, for Your servant listens."

God told Samuel that Eli and his sons would soon be punished, just as the prophet had said.

When morning came Samuel hated to tell Eli what the Lord had said. Finally, Eli called the boy to him. Samuel came as he had during the night. "Here I am," he said.

"What did the Lord tell you?" Eli asked. "Do not hide it from me." And Samuel told him the words of the Lord.

Eli bowed his head and said, "Let the Lord do what He sees is best."

David and Goliath

1 Samuel 17:1-54

David was at home caring for his father's sheep. Three of Jesse's sons were in Saul's army, and Jesse wanted to know how they were getting along. He called David from the field and told him, "Take this corn and these ten loaves of bread to your brothers and give these cheeses to their captain. Find out how your brothers are getting along. Then come back and tell me."

Early the next morning David started to the camp of Israel. When he arrived the soldiers were standing in line

for battle. At once David ran to find his brothers. As he talked to them, he noticed how the soldiers' faces grew pale in fear as they looked toward the Philistines' camp.

David wondered, "What can this mean?" Then he saw the huge giant Goliath and heard his loud shouts. He saw Saul's soldiers turn and run like frightened sheep.

The men told David about Goliath. Every morning and evening Goliath called to the Israelite soldiers. Every morning and evening the men of Israel trembled when they saw the giant and heard his mighty voice. Forty days passed and still no one would fight with him.

"Have you noticed what a giant he is? If a man kills Goliath, the king will give him riches and let him marry his daughter. King Saul has even promised to pay the debts the man's father owes." Even with such a reward, no one would fight with the giant.

David said, "Why should this wicked Philistine bother us? I will go out and kill him."

How surprised the soldiers were when they heard that! Again they told him how terrible Goliath was. Still David did not back down. The soldiers ran to tell the king.

When David was brought to the king, he said, "Don't let anyone be afraid of Goliath. I will fight him."

Saul looked at the young shepherd who stood before him. "You cannot fight against this Philistine," Saul said. "You are just a young man, and he has had long years of experience in battle."

David told the king, "I take care of my father's sheep. At different times a lion and a bear grabbed a lamb out of the flock. Both times, I rescued the lamb and killed the wild animal. This Philistine giant will be just like one of those wild animals. The Lord who helps me protect my sheep will help me defeat this Philistine."

When Saul heard this, he said to David, "Go, and the Lord be with you."

Since David was wearing the clothes of a shepherd, Saul gave his own armor to him. The brass helmet was put on David's head. The heavy metal coat was fastened around him. A sword was placed in his hand. But David could not move in this heavy armor.

He told Saul, "I cannot wear these. I am not used to them." He took off the armor and put on his own clothes. Then he went to meet Goliath.

At the brook he bent down and picked up five smooth stones. These he put in his shepherd's bag. Taking out his sling, he walked toward the giant.

How surprised Goliath was when he saw David coming toward him without a weapon! Were the Israelites making fun of him by sending this young man? Goliath roared out, "Am I a dog that you come to fight me with a stick?"

David did not turn back. Instead he called out, "You come against me with a sword, spear and shield, but I come against you in the name of the Lord."

The giant in his heavy armor moved slowly toward David. David took a stone out of his bag and ran toward Goliath. David put the stone in his sling and threw it. The stone hit the giant on the forehead, and he fell to the earth with a loud thud.

The Philistines did not wait to see more. They knew God was against them, and they left their tents and belongings behind and ran as fast as they could go. Saul's army chased after them.

There was great rejoicing among the men of Israel. They knew God had delivered them from their strong enemies.

Jonah and the Big Fish

Jonah 1—4

God spoke to Jonah and said, "Get up and go to Nineveh. Preach to the people and warn them to turn from their wickedness."

But Jonah did not want to go to Nineveh. Jonah knew the people worshiped idols. They did not know about the true God, and each year they became more wicked. Jonah could go and teach them about the true God. Instead he decided, "I'm not going to Nineveh. I'll go down to the Great Sea and take a ship going in the opposite direction. Then maybe I can get far enough away from God that He will not remind me to go to preach to the wicked Ninevites."

Down by the sea, Jonah found a ship ready to sail. He paid his fare and climbed aboard. The ship was bound for

Tarshish. Jonah was glad to be going somewhere far from Nineveh. He went down into the ship and soon fell asleep.

The ship set sail. When it got out to sea, a great storm arose. The sailors were afraid. To lighten the ship they threw all the cargo overboard. Even this did not help. Then the captain thought of Jonah. He found him below deck, sound asleep. He shook Jonah and said, "Get up! Call on God. If God doesn't save us, we will all die."

Jonah did not want to ask God for help. He knew he had disobeyed God. When he saw the mighty waves dash against the ship, he was afraid he would never see dry land again.

The sailors soon decided someone on the ship was to blame for the storm. They gathered around Jonah and asked, "Who are you and why are you on this ship?"

Jonah told them that he had run away from God.

"What can we do to calm this storm?" the men asked. They knew the ship would not hold together much longer.

"Throw me overboard and the storm will end," Jonah told them.

First the sailors tried to row toward land, but it was no use. Finally they picked Jonah up and threw him into the water. Then the waves grew quiet, the wind calmed and the storm was over.

When Jonah fell into the water, a great fish that God had made swallowed him. For three days and three nights, Jonah lived inside the fish.

During that time Jonah prayed to the Lord. He was sorry he had disobeyed. He would go to Nineveh gladly and preach to the people.

The Lord heard Jonah's prayer and had the fish cast Jonah up on the shore.

At last Jonah went to Nineveh. He told the people they would be punished because they had sinned against God. As Jonah stood on the street corners and preached, the people stopped to hear his strange message. They had never seen a prophet of God before. Some ran to tell their king what Jonah had said.

Even the king was frightened. He left his throne and took off his rich robes. He dressed in sackcloth and sat in ashes to show how sorry he was for his sins. The king said, "Let everyone dress in sackcloth and turn away from evil. Maybe God will have mercy on us and spare our lives."

After Jonah finished preaching, he went outside the city walls and waited to see fire fall on Nineveh. Although Jonah had obeyed God by telling the people of their sins, he did not want them to repent.

For forty days Jonah waited and no fire fell. Because the people believed Jonah's message and repented of their sins,

God did not destroy the city. How unhappy Jonah was! He even prayed to die.

In the night God caused a gourd vine to grow up. It grew fast and soon shaded Jonah from the burning sun. The next night a worm attacked the vine. The green leaves withered and died. Again Jonah wished he were dead.

God said to him, "You were sorry to see the plant die even though you did not make it grow. Should you not feel more sorry for the people of Nineveh than you do for a plant?"

At last Jonah understood that God loves all people.

Daniel in the Lions' Den

Daniel 6

King Darius chose many princes and three presidents to help him rule his kingdom. Because Daniel was so very wise, the king made him the first president.

The princes and the other two presidents were jealous of Daniel. They watched him carefully. They wanted to catch him doing something wrong so they could tell the king. As hard as they tried, they could not find anything to report. Finally they decided, "The only way we can find fault with him is in the way he obeys the laws of his God."

The men went to the king. "King Darius, live forever," they said. The king asked why they had come and they replied, "We have met and decided on a law you should make. For the next thirty days have every person make his requests only to you. Anyone who makes a request of any god or man except you, O King, will be thrown into the lions' den. Make this law so it cannot be changed."

Daniel had not helped plan this new law. He was not even with the group that stood before the king, but the king did not realize this. He liked being the most important person in the entire kingdom and so he signed the law. Then it was announced among all the people.

Daniel heard about the law, but he did not obey it. Just as before he knelt three times every day and prayed by his window opened toward Jerusalem. Here the other men found him on his knees thanking God.

At last they had a way to get rid of Daniel. Quickly, they hurried to the king and reminded him, "Haven't you signed a law that for thirty days every person who asks a request of any god or man except you will be thrown into the lions' den?"

"That's right," the king answered, "and that law cannot be changed."

Then the nobles told the king, "Daniel is not loyal to you, O King. He has not obeyed your law. Three times today he has prayed to his God."

How upset the king was! Now he was very sorry he had listened to the men and made such a law. All day he tried to think of some way to save Daniel.

When the sun went down, the men hurried to the palace and reminded the king that his new law had to be obeyed. Darius knew now that he could not save Daniel. He ordered him to be thrown into the lions' den.

The king told Daniel how sorry he was to do this. "The God you serve so faithfully will surely save you from the lions," the king said.

A stone was rolled over the lions' den. The king put his seal on the stone so no one would dare move it without his permission.

With a sad heart the king returned to his palace. He refused to eat any food or listen to music. Darius was so troubled that he could not sleep all night long. He kept thinking about Daniel.

In the morning King Darius hurried to the lions' den. In a worried voice he called out, "Daniel, has your God saved you from the lions?"

The king listened. From the deep pit he heard Daniel answer, "O King, live forever. My God sent His angel to shut the lions' mouths, and they did not harm me. God knew I had done no wrong."

How glad the king was! He called his servants to pull Daniel out. Then he commanded that those who had plotted against Daniel be thrown into the den.

Darius wrote letters to the people of every nation. He said, "Peace be with you. I make a law that in every part of my kingdom men shall fear Daniel's God. He is the living God, steadfast forever. His kingdom will never be destroyed, and His rule will not end. By His power He has delivered Daniel from the lions."

From that time on Daniel was treated well by the kings of Babylon.

Brave Queen Esther

Esther 1—10

Esther was only a little girl when both her parents died. Her cousin Mordecai took her to live with him, and Esther became like a daughter to him. He worked in the king's household to earn their living. Both Mordecai and Esther were Jews.

Now King Ahasuerus decided to choose another beautiful queen. Mordecai knew Esther was very beautiful. He believed she would make a good queen. When the young women came from all parts of the kingdom to the palace, Mordecai sent Esther too. He advised her, "Don't tell anyone we are related or that you are a Jew."

The king took a long time to decide on the new queen. When Esther was brought to him, he knew at once that she was the one he wanted. Ahasuerus placed the royal crown on Esther's head.

Among the princes at the royal palace was proud Haman. He was very rich and clever so the king put Haman in charge of all the princes and commanded the servants to bow to him.

When Haman passed through the king's gates, all the servants except Mordecai bowed down. Mordecai refused to bow before any man and give him the honor that belonged to God.

The next time Haman passed through the king's gate he watched Mordecai. How angry he was that this man did not bow! He must find some way to punish him. Haman decided not to punish Mordecai only, but to have all the Jews in the kingdom killed. Little did he know that Queen Esther was a Jew.

Ahasuerus did not know much about the Jews or their strange religion. He did not even know that his own wife was a Jew. He gave permission for Haman to write letters to the rulers of every part of the kingdom, announcing that all Jews were to be killed on a certain day. Royal messengers carried these letters throughout the kingdom. Haman thought he would surely get even with Mordecai now.

Esther always watched for Mordecai to pass her window each day. Then one day he did not come. What could be wrong? Quickly she sent her servant to find out. Mordecai told the servant about Haman's plan to kill all the Jews.

The servant gave Esther Mordecai's message: "If you do not go to the king, who knows what will happen? Who knows, perhaps you have come to the kingdom for such a time as this!"

Esther was afraid, but she longed to help her people. She asked Mordecai to have all the Jews pray to God for her.

On the third day Esther dressed in her most beautiful robes and went to see the king. How surprised he was to look up and see Esther standing in the court before his throne. He knew she would not have come without an important reason. Because he loved her, he held out the golden scepter that was in his hand.

Esther knelt before the throne and touched the scepter.

"What is your request, Queen Esther?" he asked. "I will give you anything you ask up to the half of my kingdom."

Esther said, "O King, please come to a special dinner that I will have for you and Haman. Then I will tell you my request."

The king promised they would come.

The king and Haman came to the dinner Esther had arranged. Again the king asked, "What would you like me to do, Queen Esther?"

Bravely the queen answered, "O King, please save my life and the lives of my people. We are all about to be killed."

Ahasuerus was shocked to hear this. He asked, "Who would dare to do such a thing?"

"The man is Haman," the queen answered.

The king ordered for Haman to be killed. Then he made Mordecai a man of great honor in the kingdom. To make sure the Jews were not killed, the king sent new letters to every part of the land.

The Jews were saved. To celebrate the day of their great victory, an important feast was held. They called it the Feast of Purim. Even to this day the Jews keep this feast and tell the story of beautiful Queen Esther who saved the lives of her people.

Jesus Is Born

Luke 2:1-39, Matthew 2

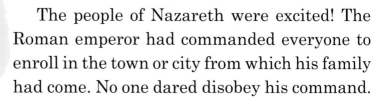

The people of Nazareth were excited! The Roman emperor had commanded everyone to enroll in the town or city from which his family had come. No one dared disobey his command.

Soon travelers were going in every direction. Joseph and Mary were going to Bethlehem, for they were both of the family of David.

When they reached Bethlehem, it was crowded with people. No place could be found for new arrivals. The journey from Nazareth had been long and hard. How much Mary wanted a place to rest! Joseph could find only the stable of the inn. That night Baby Jesus was born. Mary wrapped Him in soft cloths called swaddling clothes and laid Him in a manger.

Shepherds were watching their flocks that night near Bethlehem. Suddenly the angel of the Lord came near, and a great light shone through the darkness. The shepherds were afraid. Why had the angel come to them?

The angel said, "Don't be afraid, for I bring you good news of great joy, which will be for all people. Today a Savior has been born for you. He is Christ the Lord. And you will find the baby wrapped in swaddling clothes, lying in a manger."

What wonderful news! Many angels sang, "Glory to God in the highest, and on earth peace, good will toward men." Then the angels returned to heaven, and the light faded into the still darkness of the night.

The shepherds said to each other, "Let's go to Bethlehem and see what has happened."

Leaving their flocks, they hurried to Bethlehem. There in a stable they found Mary, Joseph and Jesus. Kneeling before the manger, they worshiped the little baby who lay quietly sleeping on the hay.

Far to the east of Judea lived certain Wise Men who studied the stars. One night they discovered a new star. By this God showed them Christ had been born.

These Wise Men loved God, and they wanted to see the child who was born to be the Savior of the world. At once they planned to take rich gifts and go to worship Him.

Many days they traveled across the desert to Judea. They hurried to Jerusalem, for surely the wonderful child would be in the most beautiful and famous city.

Herod, the ruler, was troubled. Why were these strangers riding on camels into his city? Why did they ask, "Where is He that is born king of the Jews? We have seen His star in the east and have come to worship Him."

Herod knew nothing about the newborn king. *What can this mean?* he wondered.

The chief priests and scribes remembered what the prophets had written long ago. They answered, "The Savior is to be born in Bethlehem. He is to rule His people."

Now Herod was more worried. What if this new king took away his throne? Herod told the Wise Men, "Go to Bethlehem and search for the young child. When you have found Him, let me know so I can come and worship Him."

Outside the city gates, the Wise Men saw the same bright star they had seen in the east country. It seemed to lead them. Surely God was helping them find Jesus.

At Bethlehem the star stood still over the place where

Jesus was. At last they had found Him! Falling to their knees, they worshiped Him. Opening their treasures, they gave Him rich gifts—gold, frankincense and myrrh.

Before the Wise Men left Bethlehem, God told them in a dream not to go back to Herod. So they returned to their own country by another road.

Not long afterwards, an angel of the Lord said to Joseph in a dream, "Arise, and take the young child and His mother, and flee to Egypt. Stay there until I tell you to return, for Herod will look for Jesus and try to kill Him." Joseph got up, took Mary and Jesus and hurried out of Bethlehem. They traveled until they came to Egypt.

Herod waited a long time for the Wise Men to return from Bethlehem, but they never came. Maybe they had guessed why he had been so eager to see Jesus. Now Herod was angry! He sent his soldiers to kill every child two years old or less in Bethlehem and the country round about. Surely, this would get rid of Jesus!

But Jesus was safe in Egypt. When Herod died, an angel told Joseph, "Go now and take the young child and His mother home."

Back to Bethlehem they started. In Judea Joseph learned that Herod's son was now ruler. What if the new king were like his father? Because Joseph was afraid, they went on to Nazareth. Here they made their home, and Joseph opened his carpenter's shop.

When Jesus Was a Boy

Luke 2:40-52

As a little boy, Jesus loved to watch Joseph work and to play with the shavings that fell from his bench. Of course Jesus liked to run and play outdoors with His friends too.

When Jesus was old enough to go to school, Mary and Joseph sent Him to the synagogue. Jewish boys learned to read and write there. They studied the psalms and the writings of Moses and the prophets. Like other Jewish boys, Jesus learned many Scripture verses by memory, for no one had a Bible of his own.

One spring morning a group of Jews left Nazareth for the Feast of the Passover at Jerusalem. Joseph and Mary had gone to this feast every year, but the feast would be different for them this year. They were taking Jesus for the first time. Now that Jesus was twelve, He would be going every year.

As the group moved slowly down the road, people from other cities and villages joined them. At Jerusalem they met people from every part of the land. What an exciting time this was! How wide Jesus' eyes must have been when He saw the beautiful temple!

Jesus began to understand that God was His Father and that He must work with God. Each day at the temple He listened to the chief priests and scribes and asked them questions.

After the feast the people of Nazareth started home. Mary did not see Jesus, but she thought He was with their friends and relatives.

Evening came and still Mary did not see Jesus. Joseph and she began to search for Him. They asked everyone in their group, "Have you seen Jesus?" Always the answer was the same. No one had seen Him that day.

Now Mary and Joseph were very worried. They turned back to Jerusalem, hunting for Jesus.

On the third day they found Him. He was not playing with other boys in the streets or learning to swim in the Pool of Siloam. Jesus was at the temple with the wise teachers, listening to them and asking questions.

How surprised Mary was to find Jesus there! She said, "Son, why did You stay here when we were starting for home? Your father and I have been so worried! We've looked everywhere for You."

Jesus answered, "Why did you look for Me? Didn't you know that I would be at My Father's house?" Mary did not understand. What did Jesus mean?

Jesus had surprised the teachers in the temple. He asked questions they could not answer.

As the years passed Jesus grew to be a fine young man. He learned to explain the Scriptures and to talk with

God. By helping Joseph with his work, Jesus also became a carpenter. When Joseph died, Jesus worked to care for Mary and His brothers and sisters. His kind, thoughtful ways won Him many friends. Jesus lived in His Nazareth home until He was about thirty years old.

A Boy's Lunch Basket

Matthew 14:13-23; Mark 6:30-46,
Luke 9:10-17; John 6:1-15

More and more people heard about Jesus and His miracles. They came from everywhere to hear Him teach and to have their loved ones healed. Jesus did not have time to rest or even to eat. One day Jesus called His twelve disciples to Him and said, "Come with Me to a quiet place, for we must rest awhile."

They sailed to the other side of the sea and went into a desert place. But they did not find much time to rest, for soon a great crowd gathered. The people had followed them. Maybe the disciples were disappointed because the people had found them again, but Jesus looked at the people

lovingly. "They are like sheep that have no shepherd," He said. Jesus sat down to teach them again. He healed the sick and taught the people about the kingdom of heaven.

Evening came. Still the people stayed. They seemed to forget they could not find food or shelter in the desert. The disciples wanted Jesus to send the people away.

"Send the people away," said the disciples, "so they can buy food in the towns and villages as they go home."

But Jesus answered, "We must feed them before sending them away." Turning to Philip, He asked, "Where will we find bread for all of these people to eat?"

Philip looked at the people and shook his head. "If we bought two hundred pennyworth of bread," he answered, "there would not be enough for each one to have a small piece."

In this large crowd were five thousand men besides all the women and children. When they left home, they did not know they would have to go so far to find Jesus. One boy, however, had not forgotten his lunch basket. In it were five little loaves of barley bread and two small fish.

The boy heard Jesus and the disciples talking about what to do. He went up to Andrew, showed his lunch basket and offered to give the food to Jesus. Andrew told Jesus about the boy's offer.

"How many loaves are there in the basket?" asked Jesus.

"Only five and two small fish," Andrew said. "But what will that be among so many people?"

"Bring it to Me," Jesus replied. To the disciples He said, "Make the people sit down in groups of fifty and a hundred."

Jesus took the loaves and fish, gave thanks and broke the food into small pieces. He filled a basket for each disciple to pass among the hungry people.

When the crowd had eaten all they wanted, Jesus had the disciples gather up the food that was left. There were twelve baskets full.

Jesus Blesses the Little Children
Matthew 19:13-15; Mark 10:13-16

While Jesus was teaching the people, mothers brought their little children. These mothers wanted Jesus to put His hands on the children and pray for them.

When the disciples saw the mothers and children, they did not like it. Because they thought Jesus was too busy to be bothered with little children, they called the mothers aside and said, "You should not trouble the Master with your children. He has more important work to do."

How disappointed the mothers and children were! They wanted to see Jesus and talk to Him. Maybe some had come a long way.

Just then Jesus saw the mothers and children. He called the children to Him. Jesus felt sorry for what the disciples had done. Looking at them He said, "Do not forbid the little children to come to Me, for of such is the kingdom of God. Whoever of you does not receive the kingdom of God just like a little child can never enter into it." And He took the little ones in His arms to love them.

Zacchaeus Climbs a Tree
Luke 19:1-10

In Jericho lived a rich man named Zacchaeus, who was the head tax collector. When news came that Jesus was passing through Jericho on His way to Jerusalem, Zacchaeus wanted more than anything else to see this wonderful man.

Zacchaeus stood with the crowd gathered beside the road, but he could see nothing. He was too short to see over the heads of the people. Down the road he ran and climbed into a sycamore tree. Now he could surely see Jesus.

Soon travelers going to Jerusalem came along the road. The people of Jericho watched eagerly to catch a glimpse of Jesus. When they came to the sycamore tree, Jesus and His disciples stopped. Jesus looked up and saw Zacchaeus.

"Zacchaeus," called Jesus, "come down at once, for today I must stop at your house."

How surprised Zacchaeus was! Now he could take Jesus home and talk with Him.

Joyfully Zacchaeus led the way. As they went, others followed. Some people thought Jesus should not be going to the house of a sinful man.

But Zacchaeus' heart was changed by Jesus' kind words. He told Jesus, "Lord, I will give half of my goods to the poor. And if I have taken more from anyone than I should, I will give back four times as much as I took."

Jesus was glad to hear Zacchaeus say that. Jesus answered, "Today salvation has come to your house, for the Son of man has come to seek and to save those who are lost."

Jesus Rides into Jerusalem as King

Matthew 21:1-11; Mark 11:1-11;
Luke 19:29-40; John 12:12-19

All Jerusalem was excited. People flocked out the city gate and hurried along the road. They wanted to meet Jesus because they had heard so much about Him.

As Jesus and His disciples came near to Jerusalem, He said to two of them, "Go to the village nearby. There you will see a colt that has never been ridden. Untie him and bring him to Me. If anyone asks, 'Why do you do this?' say, 'The Lord has need of him.' "

The disciples brought the colt to Jesus and spread their coats on its back. Then Jesus sat on the colt. Many people spread their clothes along the road for Jesus to ride over. Others waved palm branches. They shouted, "Blessed is the King who is coming in the name of the Lord!" As Jesus rode up to the temple, the people shouted, "Hosanna to the Son of David!"

The city people hurried into the streets to ask, "Who is this?"

The crowd answered, "This is Jesus, the prophet from Nazareth of Galilee."

Judas Betrays Jesus

Matthew 26:14-16, 36-75; Mark 14:10-11, 32-72;
Luke 22:1-6, 39-71; John 18:1-27

The chief priests hated Jesus. They wanted to kill Him. Judas, one of Jesus' disciples, went to them and asked, "What will you give me if I turn Jesus over to you?" And they promised him thirty pieces of silver.

After leaving the upper room, Jesus and the other disciples had gone to the Garden of Gethsemane. At the entrance Jesus told eight disciples, "Stay here while I go and pray." Taking Peter, James and John, He went into the garden.

While He prayed the disciples fell asleep. They could not understand why He was so troubled, and they did not know how to comfort Him. How He longed to have them near to pray with Him! Twice Jesus awakened Peter, James and John. Then while He prayed all alone, God sent an angel to strengthen and comfort Him.

63

Jesus knew He would die on the cross. He must bear the sins of the world in order to become our Savior. Because He had a body and mind like ours, He dreaded to suffer pain and to be left alone by those He loved. So He prayed, "Father, if it is possible, let this pass away from Me. Nevertheless not My will but Yours be done."

A third time Jesus woke the sleeping disciples, saying, "Get up, we must go; My betrayer is near." They followed. Soon they saw Judas with some men carrying torches. Stepping forward he said, "Hail, Master!" and kissed Jesus on the cheek.

Judas had told the men he would kiss Jesus so they would know whom to take prisoner. Taking hold of Jesus roughly, the soldiers led Him away.

The Darkest Day in All the World

Matthew 27:1-54; Mark 15:1-39, Luke 23:1-47; John 18:28—19:30

Soldiers led Jesus before the Roman governor, Pilate, who knew nothing about Jesus. Pilate took Him into the judgment hall and talked with Him. Afterwards he said, "I find no fault in this man." But the leaders stirred up the mob to shout, "Crucify Him! Crucify Him!"

Pilate was afraid. Because Pilate wanted to please the people, he called Roman soldiers and told them to lead Jesus away to be crucified. So the trial came to an end.

The Roman soldiers took Jesus and put a crown of thorns on His head. They dressed Jesus in a purple robe like a king would wear. Then they laughed and made fun of Him and hit Him. Jesus said not a word. Finally the soldiers dressed Him in His own clothes and led Him away to be crucified. They gave Jesus a heavy cross to carry.

On the hillside of Calvary soldiers fastened Jesus' hands and feet to the cross. Then they raised the cross high in the air and planted it firmly in the ground, leaving Jesus to hang there until He died.

From the cross Jesus prayed, "Father, forgive them, for they don't know what they are doing."

A sign above Jesus' head read, "This is Jesus, the King of the Jews."

Sad friends were standing at the foot of Jesus' cross. Among them were His mother and John. Jesus asked John to care for Mary.

Jesus' enemies also stood around the cross. Some of them said, "If You are the King of the Jews, save Yourself."

About noon the sky suddenly grew dark. For three hours the great darkness lasted. Then Jesus cried with a loud voice, saying, "It is finished!"

The Roman captain standing near the cross said to his soldiers, "Truly this man was the Son of God."

Jesus Rises from the Dead

Matthew 28:1-15; Mark 16:1-11; Luke 24:1-12;
John 20:1-18

The hours dragged slowly for the Roman soldiers who guarded Jesus' grave. But as dawn came the ground began to tremble. Another earthquake had come. The frightened soldiers saw a mighty angel come down, roll the stone from the grave and sit on it. The soldiers fell to the ground and lay there as if they were dead. As soon as they were able, they fled into the city to report to Jesus' enemies.

When the women came to the garden, they found the grave empty. At first they did not see the angel, and they wondered who had stolen the body of their Lord. Mary Magdalene ran to tell Peter and John that Jesus' body had been taken away.

After Mary had gone, the other women saw an angel in the tomb. They were afraid and bowed themselves to the ground.

The angel said, "Do not be afraid. Why are you seeking the living among the dead? Jesus is not here; He is risen as He said."

The women ran from the place, filled with joy, yet trembling with excitement and fear. The good news seemed too wonderful to be true. Still, they believed and hurried to tell the disciples and other friends.

The disciples could not believe the women's message. Peter and John ran to see for themselves. When they came to the tomb, they found no one, but they saw the grave clothes that had been wrapped around Jesus' body. Peter and John were sure now that Jesus was alive once more.

Welcome to the *Egermeier's*® Family!

You purchased this book because you understand the importance of introducing your child to the Word of God at an early age. It doesn't have to stop here!

For over 80 years, children, youth, and even adults worldwide have enjoyed learning from *Egermeier's*® *Bible Story Books*. As your child grows, there is an Egermeier book just right for his or her needs.

Just take a look!

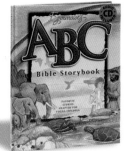

Egermeier's® ABC Bible Storybook & Audio CD
by Elsie Egermeier / Illustrated by Laura Nikiel

This delightful book uses each letter of the alphabet to highlight some of the best-loved stories in the Bible. Captivating illustrations combine with Elsie Egermeier's text to create a collection of stories that will be read over and over again. On the enclosed CD, soft music underscores the reading of the storybook to create an audio book of stories that children will keep in their hearts for a lifetime. Ages 2-5 • 9781593171988 • 8½" x 11"

Egermeier's® Bible Story Book
by Elsie Egermeier / Illustrated by Clive Upton

Beloved for generations, this classic Bible storybook has sold millions of copies and continues to bring Bible stories to life for children and adults around the world. Featuring 312 stories from Genesis to Revelation and 122 full-color illustrations, *Egermeier's® Bible Story Book* presents the reader with a comprehensive but understandable text that is free of doctrinal biases. Several pages of Bible questions/answers and other Bible helps make this a wonderful learning tool as well. Available in both hardbound and paperback editions.
Ages 8+ • Hardbound: 6½" x 9½" • 648 pages • 9781593173357
Paperback: 6" x 9" • 632 pages • 9781593173364

Find these books at your local Christian retailer, visit us online at www.warnerpress.org or call 800-741-7721 for more information.

Warner Press Kids
educate • nurture • inspire

About the Author:

Elsie Egermeier had a great love for children. As a young teen, she developed an interest in writing that later became a calling from God. When she wrote the Christian classic, *Egermeier's® Bible Story Book*, she tested what she wrote by reading it to children to be sure they understood and enjoyed the stories.

About the Illustrator:

Pat Paris has illustrated over 50 books. Some clients include Disney, Hallmark Cards, Random House, and Simon Schuster.

She designed LucasFilm (*Star Wars*™) Ewoks and Sea World's "Shamu and His Crew" licensed characters. Her colorful children's illustrations are animated and fun. Pat says, "This book brought back all the wonderful memories of my religious background and the stories read to me as a child. I hope children will enjoy these stories as much as I did."